How to Play the Ocarina for Beginners

The Ultimate Guide to Learning, Playing, and Becoming Proficient at the Instrument

Table of Contents

Introduction

As you embark on the journey into the enchanting world of the ocarina, this guide is tailored to be your compass, navigating you through the essential aspects of mastering this whimsical musical instrument. With each chapter, you'll uncover valuable insights and acquire the skills to master the ocarina.

Your exploration begins with an insightful journey into the historical and cultural backdrop of the ocarina. Discover the origins and evolution of this unique instrument, understanding its place in the tapestry of civilizations across time. The first chapter sets the stage for a deeper connection with your ocarina.

Whether you're a novice or a seasoned player, the second chapter navigates the myriad options available. From materials to shapes and sizes, each consideration contributes to finding an ocarina that resonates with your musical aspirations.

As you delve into ocarina music, a solid foundation in basic music theory becomes your guide. The third chapter equips you with the essential knowledge to navigate the notes, scales, and rhythms that breathe life into your ocarina playing. This understanding lays the groundwork for a more profound musical experience.

With your ocarina in hand, the fourth chapter focuses on the practical aspects of handling the instrument. Learn the proper techniques for holding and positioning your ocarina to optimize playability and sound production. Mastering these fundamental skills ensures a seamless connection between musician and instrument.

The fifth and sixth chapters take things from the theoretical to the practical. You'll find out the intricacies and the art of learning ocarina songs. From breath control to vibrato, dynamics, and articulation, you'll unlock the secrets to infusing your music with nuance and expression. Explore the many ways the ocarina can be a vessel for your artistic voice.

Your journey extends beyond solo performances as you discover the joy of playing with others. Chapter seven provides insights into ensemble playing, guiding you on how to harmonize with fellow musicians. Whether part of a duet, trio, or larger ensemble, this chapter explores the collaborative magic of making music together.

Finally, as you ascend to higher levels of mastery, chapter eight is your guide to advancing your ocarina skills. Explore advanced techniques, delve into complex compositions, and refine your musical interpretation. This chapter is a gateway to unlocking the full potential of your ocarina-playing journey.

This book guide is crafted to be your companion, offering a roadmap to mastering the ocarina. Each chapter unfolds a new layer of understanding, providing practical advice and hands-on techniques to enhance your playing experience. Whether you're a beginner seeking foundational knowledge or an experienced player aiming to refine your skills, the following chapters welcome you to the enchanting ocarina. With curiosity as your guide and this book as your ally, let the melodious adventure begin.

Chapter 1: Background to the Ocarina

In setting the stage for an in-depth examination of the ocarina, this chapter seeks to unravel the historical tapestry surrounding this unique musical instrument. With its roots extending over millennia, the ocarina's narrative unfolds across continents and cultures, intertwining stories of invention, migration, and adaptation. You are invited to delve into the rich background of the ocarina, revealing the echoes of its ancient melodies resonating through time and space. The intention behind this exploration is to illuminate the diverse threads interweaving and forming the intricate story of the ocarina's evolution and enduring allure.

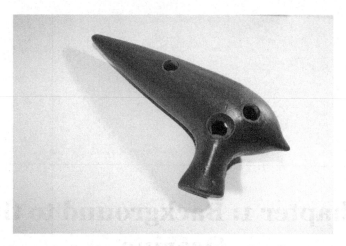

1. *The ocarina holds a unique place in the realm of music. Source: Again, taken by me., Public domain, via Wikimedia Commons: https://commons.wikimedia.org/wiki/File:Baldur_ocarina2.jpg*

What Is the Ocarina?

The ocarina, an intriguing instrument with a history as diverse as the cultures that embraced it, holds a unique place in the realm of music. Characterized by its distinctive round shape reminiscent of sweet potatoes, the ocarina has carved its niche in the musical landscape for over 12,000 years. Unlike more intricate counterparts, the ocarina's charm lies in its simplicity, making it accessible to musicians and enthusiasts. With its characteristic round form and enchanting resonance, this unassuming flute transcends geographical boundaries, traversing continents and absorbing the cultural nuances that shape its identity.

At its core, the ocarina is a cool, round flute that breathes life into melodies with a touch of magic. Crafted from various materials, including clay and wood, this timeless instrument exudes an air of ancient elegance. Its evolution, a result of centuries of travel and transformation, reflects not only changes in its appearance but also in its tonal capabilities. The ocarina embarked on a global journey from its origins in South America, where it first took shape as clay instruments resembling birds or animals. It harmonized with drums and other instruments in South America, Central America, and Mesoamerica, forming rhythmic ensembles resonating with the pulse of diverse cultures.

The ocarina's enduring appeal lies in its historical significance and in its contemporary resurgence. Despite facing shifts in popularity over time, this charming instrument has stood the test of history and modern trends. In recent decades, the ocarina's revival can be attributed, in part, to its prominent role in popular culture, notably propelled by the video game "The Legend of Zelda: Ocarina of Time." As a result, this ancient flute has once again found its way into the hearts of a global audience, proving that its timeless melodies continue to strike a chord in the ever-evolving musical landscape.

Origin of the Ocarina

Originating approximately 12,000 years ago in South America, the ocarina boasts a fascinating narrative unfolding across continents. Its humble beginnings trace back to clay instruments shaped like birds or animals, featuring holes for fingers and a mouthpiece for producing music. The simplicity of its design facilitated the ocarina's integration into various musical landscapes in South America, Central America, and Mesoamerica. The ocarinas, collaborating with drums and other instruments, contributed to creating rhythmic tunes, becoming integral components of diverse cultural expressions.

The Spread of Ocarinas to Europe during the Mexican Colonial Era

The ocarina's migratory journey gained momentum during the Mexican Colonial Era when, in 1527, Hernán Cortez returned to Spain from Mesoamerica. Accompanying him were musicians who brought artifacts from Mayan and Aztec civilizations and the enchanting sounds of the ocarina. In an unexpected turn of events, a baker in Rome witnessed these musicians playing the unfamiliar instrument and found it captivating. Inspired, crafted his version of the ocarina, setting off a chain reaction of reproductions that spread across Europe.

However, European ocarinas underwent a transformation, differing from their South American counterparts, and were initially perceived as novelty items rather than serious musical instruments. Despite this initial perception, the ocarina's journey persisted across Europe's musical landscape.

Giuseppe Donati's Ocarina

The evolution of the ocarina took a significant turn in 1852 when Giuseppe Donati, a teenager, injected new life into the instrument's simplicity. He ingeniously shaped it like a little goose, christening it the "ocarina." Donati's innovative approach extended to the materials used, incorporating clay and wood to craft these musical gems. This transformative moment in the ocarina's history was further solidified when Donati established the group GOB in 1863, propelling ocarinas into the spotlight and celebrating their unique charm. The legacy of Giuseppe Donati's creative touch continues as enthusiasts around the world gather every few years for a grand celebration, uniting ocarina fans in a collective appreciation for the instrument's enduring charm.

Modern Days

In more recent times, the ocarina has experienced fluctuations in popularity, navigating through different musical landscapes. During World War II, soldiers found solace in the melodies of pocket-sized ocarinas, but the limelight shifted with the rising fame of the recorder. However, the ocarina experienced a resurgence in popularity in 1998 when a video game titled "The Legend of Zelda: Ocarina of Time" catapulted it back into the limelight. This showcased the timeless appeal of the ocarina as people across the globe sought replicas of the instrument featured in the game. It also emphasized the instrument's ability to transcend eras, proving that even in the digital age, the enchanting notes of the ocarina can have a resounding impact on modern sensibilities.

Different Types and Styles of Ocarinas

Diverse styles and types of ocarinas are found across different epochs, each contributing to the instrument's rich tapestry of sound and design. Sculptural whistles, reminiscent of bird cries and adorned with vibrant glazes, emerged as playful novelties shaped like birds and animals. While not intended as serious instruments, these added a touch of artistry to the ocarinas.

Historically, the Pre-Columbian, Peruvian, and Mexican ocarinas raised debates about their purpose, as they seemed to mimic natural sounds like birds, insects, thunder, wind, and rustling leaves. The 'Peruvian ocarina,' a contemporary rendition, is recognized by its flat shape, painted designs, and

8 to 10 identical holes, though often criticized for poor sound quality and lack of tuning suitability for serious musicians.

The 19th century introduced the transverse ocarina, an Italian innovation resembling a shorter, rounder flute. With a fingering system akin to the recorder or flute, it achieved full chromaticity with 9 to 12 holes, paving the way for multi-chamber versions and expanding the instrument's note range. Inline ocarinas added a twist by placing the mouthpiece at the end, offering advantages for those with arthritis or wrist issues, although stability and handling challenges accompanied these benefits. The subsequent evolution saw the emergence of transverse multi-chamber ocarinas, magical combinations of smaller ocarinas attached to only a single one, providing a versatile and expressive musical experience. With their distinct finger holes and tuning systems, these multi-chambered instruments opened up new possibilities for those seeking a broader range of notes.

Sculptural Whistles:

The world of ocarinas boasts the charming presence of sculptural whistles, delightful novelties that mimic bird sounds, and more. These artistic creations go beyond mere instruments, shaped like birds and animals adorned with colorful glazes that turn them into visual delights. While sculptural whistles may not be crafted with the seriousness of traditional instruments in mind, their playful designs add a unique and artistic touch to the ocarinas.

Pre-Columbian, Peruvian, and Mexican Ocarinas:

2. *Mexican toad ocarina. Source: Los Angeles County Museum of Art,*
Public domain, via Wikimedia Commons:
https://commons.wikimedia.org/wiki/File:Toad_Ocarina.jpg

Delving into history, the purpose of pre-Columbian, Peruvian, and Mexican ocarinas remains a subject of debate. With shapes echoing nature, these ancient instruments imitated sounds like birds, insects, thunder, wind, and rustling leaves. The contemporary rendition, known as the 'Peruvian ocarina,' inherits a flat shape, painted designs, and

8 to 10 identical holes. Despite the recognition, criticism often surrounds these replicas for their weak sound quality and lack of tuning, which renders them less suitable for serious musicians looking for precision.

Transverse Ocarinas:

In the 19th century, Italian ingenuity birthed the transverse ocarina, a remarkable instrument resembling a shorter, rounder flute. Held like a flute but possessing a fingering system akin to the recorder, this innovation achieved full chromaticity with 9 to 12 holes. The advent of multi-chamber versions expanded the ocarina's musical range, allowing musicians to explore a broader spectrum of notes. As the ocarina evolved, inline versions emerged, retaining the traditional finger holes but placing the mouthpiece at the end for a unique playing experience. While these inline ocarinas offered advantages for individuals with arthritis or wrist issues, they also introduced challenges related to stability and handling.

Transverse Multi-Chamber Ocarinas:

This enchanting creation combines several smaller ocarinas into a single instrument, and each chamber is tuned to perfection. Available in double, triple, or quadruple variations, these ocarinas provide a broader range of notes, allowing more expressive musical compositions. Unlike their single-chamber counterparts, transverse multi-chamber ocarinas are not classified by the number of holes but by the number of chambers they possess. Musicians venturing into this realm must consult the manufacturer's fingering chart to navigate the unique finger holes and specific tuning system of each chamber, unlocking the full potential of this versatile and expressive instrument.

Xuns:

3. *The Xun is a distinctive Chinese instrument. Source: Metropolitan Museum of Art, CCo, via Wikimedia Commons: https://commons.wikimedia.org/wiki/File:Xun_MET_DP169485.j pg*

The Xun, a distinctive Chinese instrument, sets itself apart with its flute-like blowhole, deviating from the conventional ducted voicing of other ocarinas. Pronounced 'shoon,' the Xun carries its own playing tradition, accompanied by various fingering systems. While it facilitates expressive playing, coaxing sound from the Xun demands precision in controlling the airstream. Rooted in traditional Chinese heritage, the Xun has a captivating touch of mystery, adding an intriguing dimension to the diverse world of ocarinas.

Microtonal Ocarinas:

The Microtonal Ocarina, an innovation by Wesley Hicks, presents a unique musical instrument distinguished by one or two large holes covered by the player's palms. This distinctive design empowers the Microtonal Ocarina to navigate Western chromatic scales or scales from diverse musical traditions. The key to its distinction lies in the player's ability to hear and meticulously adjust the pitch, elevating the importance of attentive listening. What sets these ocarinas apart is their remarkable control over pitch and volume. By manipulating the openness of the holes, players can craft soft tones or amplify volume with intensified blowing. It makes playing more intuitive than conventional transverse ocarinas. With its precision and versatility, the Microtonal Ocarina stands as a testament to the evolving landscape of ocarina craftsmanship and musical exploration.

Chapter 2: Choosing Your Ocarina

Choosing the right ocarina can be a bit like finding the perfect pair of shoes - it needs to fit just right for a great experience. This chapter will cover everything you need to know to pick the right ocarina. It will guide you toward the instrument that feels like an extension of your musical self. Whether you're a musical prodigy or just starting to dip your toes into the vast world of instruments, this chapter promises to be your compass by including how to select the right ocarina and the various materials and sizes available.

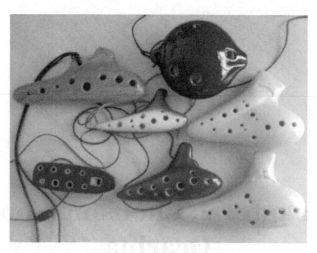

4. Choosing the right ocarina for you is the first step towards mastering the instrument. Source: Samuel Lee, Public domain, via Wikimedia Commons: https://commons.wikimedia.org/wiki/File:Ocarina_family.jpg

Selecting the Right Ocarina for You

Selecting the right ocarina involves four key considerations:

1. Skill Level:

When diving into the world of ocarinas, assessing your skill level is the first step toward finding the perfect fit. For beginners, a 12-hole ocarina in the key of C is recommended. This choice is not only user-friendly but is also widely integrated into learning materials, providing a supportive foundation for novice players to build their musical skills. Exploring ocarinas with additional holes or in different keys can provide a broader range of possibilities for more advanced players.

2. Ocarina Styles:

The vast array of ocarina styles invites exploration, and understanding these variations can significantly enhance your experience. Consider if you're captivated by the sweet, ethereal sounds of a pendant ocarina or lean toward the more robust tones of a transverse ocarina. Your preferred style will act as a guiding force, leading you to the instrument that harmonizes best with your musical spirit.

3. Budgeting for Quality:

Budget considerations play a pivotal role in the ocarina selection process. While a top-of-the-line model may not be a necessity for beginners, a slightly higher investment often translates to a better-quality instrument. View this expenditure as a musical investment in your melodic future, recognizing that a well-crafted ocarina can significantly contribute to the richness of your musical experience.

4. Aesthetics:

The visual allure of an ocarina should not be underestimated, as it can be a powerful motivator during practice sessions. Whether you are drawn to the timeless charm of a classic, elegant design or prefer the whimsy of a vibrant, colorful choice, seek an ocarina that resonates with you on a personal level. The aesthetics of your chosen instrument can elevate the joy of playing and inspire you to engage in your musical endeavors with heightened enthusiasm.

Selecting the right ocarina involves thoughtful consideration of your skill level, an exploration of different styles, a budget-conscious approach, and an appreciation for the visual aesthetics that personally inspire and motivate you. By carefully navigating these aspects, you'll find an ocarina that not only fits you perfectly but also enhances your musical experience.

The Main Types of Ocarinas

1. 10-Hole Ocarina:

The 10-hole ocarina is a popular choice characterized by its teardrop shape and versatile design. With ten finger holes and available in various keys, it caters to players of different skill levels. Commonly chosen by beginners and intermediate players, the 10-hole ocarina is capable of producing a wide range of musical genres, making it a well-rounded and accessible option.

2. 12-Hole Ocarina:

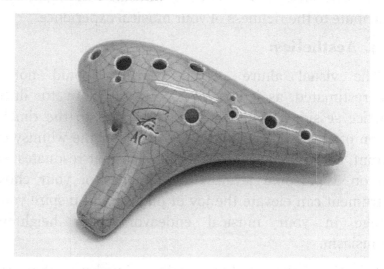

5.   12-hole ocarina. Source: 0x010C, CC BY-SA 4.0 <https://creativecommons.org/licenses/by-sa/4.0>, via Wikimedia Commons: https://commons.wikimedia.org/wiki/File:2016-01_Ocarina_front.jpg

Similar in shape to the 10-hole counterpart, the 12-hole ocarina is distinguished by its extended tonal range. The addition of two extra holes allows more complex melodies and a broader selection of playable songs. This ocarina is favored by those seeking versatility in their playing, enabling them to explore a wider spectrum of musical expressions compared to its 10-hole counterpart.

3. Transverse Ocarina:

Played horizontally, akin to a flute, the transverse ocarina stands out for its distinctive shape and the rich, resonant tones it produces. This type often boasts a more extensive range of notes and is favored by players looking to achieve a robust and melodious sound. The transverse ocarina offers a unique playing experience, making it a choice for those wanting a more traditional yet expressive instrument.

4. Pendant Ocarina:

Compact and portable, the pendant ocarina is designed to be worn around the neck like a piece of jewelry. Usually featuring six to ten holes, it offers a charming and ethereal sound. Despite its limited tonal range, the pendant ocarina is cherished for its portability and unique, whimsical quality, making it a popular choice for those who appreciate style and musicality.

5. Double Ocarina:

The double ocarina is a unique variation consisting of two ocarinas connected together. This design is suitable for harmonies and duet playing, providing a rich and layered sound. While mastering the double ocarina requires more advanced playing techniques, the reward lies in its intricate musical possibilities. This type is often favored by experienced players seeking to explore the complexities of dual-chambered instruments.

6. Multi-Chambered Ocarina:

Featuring multiple chambers, each equipped with its own set of finger holes, the multi-chambered ocarina opens up possibilities for playing chords or different melodies simultaneously. This design requires a high level of skill and coordination, attracting advanced players who enjoy the challenge of managing multiple chambers to create harmonious arrangements and intricate musical textures.

7. Inline Ocarina:

With a straight design resembling a recorder, the inline ocarina offers a unique playing experience. Played horizontally, it combines the traditional shape of a transverse ocarina with the straight alignment of other wind instruments. This type is known for its distinct sound and appeals to players looking for a novel approach to ocarina playing.

8. Quad Ocarina:

The quad ocarina stands out with its four chambers, providing an extensive range of notes and harmonies. Playing the quad ocarina demands advanced skills, with each chamber requiring individual attention. However, the payoff is a rich and layered musical experience, making it a preferred choice for accomplished ocarina enthusiasts seeking complexity and depth.

Understanding Ocarina Materials and Sizes

Now that you understand what goes into choosing your ocarina and the considerations you need to make, the last two things you need to keep in mind are materials and sizes. At the core of your experience are the materials, influencing not only the aesthetic but also the distinct tonal characteristics of each ocarina.

The following are the most common materials ocarinas are made from:

1. **Ceramic:** Ceramic ocarinas are timeless classics, appreciated for their smooth surfaces, intricate designs, and, most notably, their warm and resonant tones. These ocarinas, crafted from fired clay, often carry a certain elegance in their design, making them more than musical instruments but works of art. The inherent properties of ceramic contribute to a mellowness and depth in the sound, creating a harmonious experience for players and listeners. Popular among enthusiasts and collectors, ceramic ocarinas are cherished for their aesthetic appeal and the rich, emotive quality they bring to musical compositions.

2. **Plastic:** Plastic ocarinas have carved a niche for themselves in the world of musical instruments, offering a practical and affordable option for players of all levels. These ocarinas, crafted from durable polymers, are known for their lightweight construction, making them an excellent choice for those on the go. While the material may lack the natural resonance of ceramic or other alternatives, it compensates with its affordability, accessibility, and resistance to environmental factors. Plastic ocarinas are ideal entry-level instruments for beginners, schools, and players seeking a reliable and cost-effective option without compromising the joy of playing.

3. **Metal:** Metal ocarinas introduce a modern twist to the traditional instrument, bringing sleek designs and a distinct resonance to the musical scene. These ocarinas, crafted from materials like aluminum or brass, exhibit a unique tonal quality that sets them apart. Known for their bright and clear sound, metal

ocarinas often appeal to players who appreciate a contemporary aesthetic and a crisp, cutting-edge musical experience. The use of metal also allows for innovative designs and finishes, contributing to the instrument's visual appeal while maintaining a high level of durability.

4. **Wood:** While less common than other materials, wooden ocarinas offer a unique and earthy tonal quality that appeals to a specific audience. Crafted from various types of wood, each imparting its acoustic properties, wooden ocarinas can produce warm, organic tones. The wood's grain patterns and natural textures contribute to their aesthetic charm, making them prized possessions for those who appreciate the connection between natural materials and musical expression. While their use may be more niche, wooden ocarinas provide a distinctive acoustic experience that resonates with players pursuing a closer connection to nature in their music.

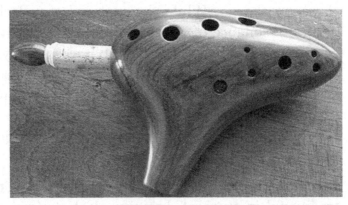

6.   *Ocarinas can be made out of wood. Source: Paolo Gavelli, Public domain, via Wikimedia Commons: https://commons.wikimedia.org/wiki/File:Ocarina_a_pistone_coc obolo.JPG*

Whether you're drawn to the classic warmth of ceramic, the versatility of plastic, the resonance of metal, or the earthy tones of wood, the choice of material is an integral part of your experience. Now, the last thing you need to think about is the size of your ocarina.

The following are the most widely available sizes:

1. **Soprano:** Soprano ocarinas are the smallest in size, often recognized for their bright and crisp tones. Their compact nature makes them ideal for beginners and players who appreciate the portability of a smaller instrument. Despite their size, soprano ocarinas can still produce a surprising range of notes.

2. **Alto Ocarinas:** Stepping up in size, the alto ocarina strikes a balance between portability and a richer tonal palette. Offering a broader range of notes than sopranos, they are favored by players who desire a more versatile instrument while maintaining a manageable size.

3. **Tenor:** Tenor ocarinas are larger and, consequently, produce deeper, more resonant tones. This size is often favored by intermediate and advanced players for its extended range and ability to handle complex musical compositions. Its size provides a satisfying heft and presence in the hands of the player.

4. **Bass:** At the larger end of the spectrum, bass ocarinas are known for their deep, rich tones. These instruments are substantial in size and require a more significant breath control technique. Often chosen for their ability to anchor the lower register in ensemble playing, bass ocarinas contribute a robust foundation to musical arrangements.

5. **Multi-Octave:** Some ocarinas are designed with multiple chambers or octaves, providing an extensive range of notes. While requiring advanced playing skills, these instruments offer unparalleled versatility, enabling players to cover a wide range of pitches.

This chapter has covered everything you need to know to pick the right ocarina. If, for whatever reason, you're still hesitant, acquire some hands-on experience. When it comes to instruments, especially ones you're unfamiliar with, nothing beats the first time you get your hands on them. The next chapter will go over basic music theory for an ocarina player. Whether you have some experience or none at all, you're bound to learn something new.

Chapter 3: Basic Music Theory for Ocarina Players

This chapter's primary goal is to introduce you to fundamental music theory concepts specifically tailored for you as an ocarina player. It explains musical notation, the elements that make it up, and a few basic music theory concepts you should explore as an ocarina player.

\relative c' { c d e f | g2 g | a4 a a a | g1 |}

7.   *Musical notation is the written language of music. Source: Lea Lacroix (WMDE), CC BY-SA 4.0 <https://creativecommons.org/licenses/by-sa/4.0>, via Wikimedia Commons: https://commons.wikimedia.org/wiki/File:Screenshot_musical_no tation_Wikidata_2.png*

Navigating Musical Notation

What Is Musical Notation?

Musical notation is the written language of music. It is a system of symbols and markings musicians use to communicate and interpret musical ideas. Like written words convey meaning in language, musical notation allows composers to express their musical thoughts and performers to bring those thoughts to life. This visual representation provides a standardized way for musicians around the world to read and interpret compositions, enabling a universal language that transcends cultural and linguistic barriers.

The basic elements of musical notation include notes, representing the pitch or frequency of a sound, and various symbols indicating aspects like duration, dynamics (loudness or softness), tempo (speed), and articulation (how notes are played). The musical staff, consisting of five horizontal lines and four spaces, is the primary framework for organizing these symbols. Notes are positioned on the staff to denote their pitch. The shape of the notes determines their duration. A variety of other symbols, like clefs, key signatures, and time signatures, further refine the information presented on the staff.

Learning to read musical notation is a lot like learning a new language, and like any language, it requires practice. Beginners often start by understanding the basics of note reading, recognizing the placement of notes on the staff and their corresponding pitches. As you progress, additional elements of musical notation come into play, providing a more nuanced and expressive interpretation of the composer's intentions. With dedication and practice, you can gain access to the rich world of musical notation, opening the door to endless music.

Notes

Each note represents a specific pitch or frequency of a sound. For example, the note "G" is symbolized by a distinct marking placed on the second line of the musical staff, while "E" is positioned in the space just below.

The shape of the note conveys the duration of the sound. For example, a filled-in oval signifies a quarter note, indicating a relatively moderate duration. Different shapes and configurations, like hollow ovals with stems (eighth notes) or flags (sixteenth notes), further refine the duration associated with each note.

Musical Staff

The musical staff consists of five horizontal lines and four spaces, providing a standardized framework for organizing musical symbols. These lines and spaces are numbered from bottom to top, each representing a different pitch level.

Clefs, such as the treble clef and bass clef, are symbols placed at the beginning of the staff to specify the range of pitches. For example, the treble clef situates the note "F" on the top line, while the bass clef locates "G" on the second line from the bottom. Using clefs and the staff together allows musicians to precisely identify and understand each note's pitch.

Dynamics (Loudness or Softness)

Dynamics are symbols that convey the loudness or softness of the music. For instance, markings like "piano" (soft) and "forte" (loud) provide instructions for the musician.

The "fortissimo" marking is an extreme example, indicating a very loud performance.

Tempo (Speed of the Music)

Tempo markings indicate the speed of the music. Terms like "allegro" suggest a fast tempo, while "adagio" implies a slow pace. These markings guide performers in capturing the intended mood and character of a piece.

Articulation Marks

Articulation marks, such as staccato (short and detached) or legato (smooth and connected), specify how notes are played. These markings contribute to the overall expressiveness and interpretation of the music.

Key Signatures and Time Signatures

Key signatures indicate the tonal center and the arrangement of sharps or flats, while time signatures establish the rhythmic framework and guide the performer in beats per measure. Understanding these symbols is integral for accurately playing and interpreting musical compositions.

Essential Music Theory Concepts for Ocarina

Fingering and Pitch

Understanding the relationship between ocarina fingering and pitch is fundamental. Each hole on the ocarina produces a specific pitch, and knowing how to cover or uncover these holes correctly determines the notes you play. For example, on a 12-hole ocarina, covering all the holes produces the lowest note while gradually uncovering them increases the pitch. As you progress, explore different ocarina sizes and their corresponding fingerings. Covering the rightmost holes on a soprano ocarina produces higher pitches, while covering the leftmost holes produces lower pitches on a bass ocarina.

Scales and Modes

To familiarize yourself with common musical patterns, you need to learn major and minor scales. Scales are the sequences of notes that form the foundation of melodies. On a 6-hole ocarina, playing a major scale involves covering and uncovering specific holes in a specific order, producing a bright and uplifting sound. Experiment with modes; for instance, playing a Dorian mode on an 8-hole ocarina alters the sequence of whole and half steps, creating a unique, jazzy flavor. Understanding scales and modes enhances your ability to compose, improvise, and interpret a broader range of music on the ocarina.

Rhythm and Timing

To play engaging music, you need to master both rhythm and timing. You must familiarize yourself with time signatures and understand the organization of beats in a measure. For example, in 4/4 time, there are four beats per measure, with each quarter note having one beat. A simple exercise you can practice involves playing a basic melody using whole notes, half notes, and quarter notes on a 10-hole ocarina. A solid understanding of rhythm allows you to play music with precision and maintain a steady tempo and dynamic flow.

Dynamics and Articulation

Expressiveness in ocarina playing goes beyond hitting the right notes. Explore dynamics to understand how to control the volume of your playing, using markings like "piano" (soft) and "forte" (loud). On an 8-hole ocarina, experiment with playing a melody softly in one section and loudly in another to convey emotional contrast. Experiment with articulation, such as staccato (short and detached) or legato (smooth and connected), to shape the character of your music. Playing a familiar tune with legato articulation on a pendant ocarina produces a flowing, seamless quality, while using staccato creates a more lively and punctuated rendition. Mastering dynamics and articulation allows you to convey emotions and nuances, elevating the quality of your ocarina performances.

Once you have mastered the basics, elevate your playing with the help of these tips:

- **Use Breath Control for Expression:** Develop control over your breath to add expressiveness to your ocarina playing. Experiment with varying breath pressure to achieve different dynamics. A gentle breath produces softer notes, while a slightly stronger breath creates louder, more robust tones. This control enhances your ability to convey emotions and infuse character into your melodies.

- **Explore Ornamentation Techniques:** Techniques like trills, grace notes, and slides can add flair and personality to your playing. Experiment with these embellishments on familiar tunes to discover how they enhance your musical expression.

- **Ear Training and Pitch Accuracy:** Sharpen your ear and improve pitch accuracy by practicing with a reference pitch. Use a tuner or play with recorded music to develop a keen sense of pitch. It not only helps you stay in tune but also enhances your ability to play by ear, making it easier to learn new tunes and improvise.

- **Vary Your Playing Styles:** Keep your ocarina playing interesting by experimenting with different styles. Whether it's classical, folk, pop, or even video game music, exposing yourself to diverse genres broadens your musical palette. Explore the unique challenges and techniques associated with each style to enrich your overall playing experience.

- **Record Yourself:** Record your ocarina playing sessions and take time to listen with a critical ear. This practice allows you to identify areas for improvement, such as intonation, rhythm, and articulation. It also serves as a valuable tool for tracking your progress over time. You develop a more discerning ear and refine your musical interpretation by listening to your recordings.

- **Experiment with Tunings:** Explore ocarinas with different tunings to expand your musical palette. Ocarinas come in various tunings, including transverse, pendant, and double ocarinas. Each type offers unique tonal possibilities. Trying different tunings broadens your horizons and helps you discover the nuances and versatility of this instrument. Experimenting with various tunings can inspire creativity and open up new avenues for musical exploration.

- **Join Communities and Workshops:** Connect with fellow ocarina enthusiasts by joining online communities and forums or attending workshops. Engaging with a community provides opportunities to share experiences, exchange tips, and discover new music. Whether virtual or in-person, workshops offer valuable insights from experienced players, helping you refine your skills and broaden your understanding of the instrument. Collaborating with others can also lead to exciting musical collaborations and friendships within the ocarina community.

Before you pick up your ocarina, remember that each note played, each symbol interpreted, and each new concept embraced contributes to your growth as a musician. The language of music is universal and personal. It transcends boundaries while allowing individual voices like yours to resonate. So, practice, explore, and immerse yourself in the world of music. This next chapter will take you through handling the ocarina you picked.

Chapter 4: Handling the Ocarina

Playing the ocarina goes beyond simply hitting the right notes. This chapter serves as a practical guide and teaches you how to effectively use your breath and fingers to produce delightful music. You will find instructions on breath control and sound production. The emphasis is on simplifying the mechanics of breath control and providing actionable methods to enhance the overall sound quality your ocarina produces.

8. *To play the ocarina, you have to know how to handle it. Source: rod_waddington, CC BY-SA 2.0 <https://creativecommons.org/licenses/by-sa/2.0>, via Wikimedia Commons: https://commons.wikimedia.org/wiki/File:Amerindian_woman_p laying_an_inca_ocarina.png*

Whether you're a beginner or an experienced player looking to refine your skills, this chapter caters to individuals of all proficiency levels.

Proper Hand Positions and Fingerings

Like other instruments, the ocarina's sound depends on how well you hold it. To properly hold your ocarina, keep the following five points in mind.

Understand the Basics

Proper hand positioning is foundational for any ocarina player, and it begins with a solid grasp of the instrument. Hold it gently with both hands, allowing your thumbs to support it from below. Make sure the instrument is parallel to the ground to create a comfortable starting point for finger placement. The left-hand fingers should cover the four front holes, while the right-hand fingers cover the four back holes. This initial positioning sets the stage for effective finger control and note production.

Finger Placement

Each finger on both hands plays a specific role in covering ocarina holes, directly influencing the notes produced. The left-hand thumb usually covers the bottom back hole, and the remaining fingers take care of the other three holes. On the right hand, the thumb covers the bottom back hole, while the other fingers address the top three holes. Understanding this finger placement is essential for accurate and intentional playing, allowing you to produce clear and distinct notes.

A Relaxed Grip for Fluid Playing

Maintaining a relaxed grip is paramount for effective ocarina playing. Tension in the hands can hinder fluid movements and cause unnecessary fatigue. Focus on a light, relaxed grip that allows your fingers to move effortlessly between holes. This approach promotes smoother transitions between notes and enhances overall control. You will have longer playing sessions with relative ease by avoiding unnecessary pressure.

Developing Hand Coordination

Hand coordination is a skill that evolves through deliberate practice. Start with simple exercises that involve uncovering and covering specific holes in a sequence. Playing scales or basic tunes helps develop muscle memory and strengthens the coordination between your hands. Consistent practice will contribute to improved dexterity, enabling you to navigate the ocarina with precision and confidence.

Experimentation

As you become more proficient in basic hand positioning, it's beneficial to experiment with different fingerings. Explore alternative placements for specific notes and chords, understanding how slight adjustments can alter the sound. This experimentation not only enhances your versatility as a player but also contributes to your expressiveness.

The next step to handling the ocarina is fingering. Like hand positioning, keep the following five points in mind.

Fundamental Finger Techniques

Mastering ocarina fingerings is a crucial aspect of becoming a proficient player. Begin with a solid understanding of the basic finger techniques. Each finger corresponds to a specific hole on the ocarina, and precise finger placement is essential for producing accurate notes. Practice covering and uncovering the holes individually to build muscle memory and control over each finger's movement. This skill sets the stage for more complex fingerings and advanced playing.

As a beginner, you should master these three exercises:

- **Single-Hole Isolation**

Mastering single-hole isolation is crucial for developing precise control over each finger's movement. This exercise helps beginners familiarize themselves with the sensation of covering and uncovering individual holes on the ocarina. Start with the index finger and gradually work through each finger, ensuring the remaining holes stay securely closed. The goal is to achieve airtight seals and consistent sound production. This exercise lays the groundwork for more complex finger techniques, promoting finger strength, independence, and overall control.

- **Chromatic Scale Exercise**

The chromatic scale exercise is designed to improve dexterity and finger coordination across the ocarina's range. Begin by playing a continuous scale of half steps, covering and uncovering various combinations of holes. Focus on maintaining a steady airflow and pitch throughout the scale. This exercise is beneficial for navigating the ocarina's entire range, helping players become more comfortable with different fingerings. Players can explore more intricate chromatic patterns as proficiency increases, contributing to their overall skill development.

- **Arpeggio Patterns**

Practicing arpeggios with specific fingerings adds a musical dimension to finger technique exercises. Start with simple triads, such as the C major chord (C-E-G), and play them in ascending and descending patterns. This exercise enhances finger control and agility while reinforcing understanding of chord structures. As you progress, experiment with more complex chords, preparing you for the demands of playing diverse musical pieces. The ability to transition smoothly between different chords is a valuable skill this exercise helps cultivate.

Transitioning between Notes

Smooth transitions between notes are crucial for creating melodic and harmonious tunes. Focus on lifting and placing your fingers meticulously, ensuring a seamless flow of sound. Practice simple scales and melodic exercises, gradually increasing the complexity of the sequences. This step-by-step approach allows your fingers to adapt to the unique demands of ocarina playing and enhances your ability to navigate between different fingerings effortlessly.

Understanding the Ocarina's Range

The ocarina has a limited range of notes, and understanding the fingerings for each note within that range is essential. Familiarize yourself with the lowest and highest notes your ocarina can produce. Practice ascending and descending scales to grasp the full scope of available fingerings. This knowledge gives a solid foundation for playing various songs and allows you to explore the instrument's tonal possibilities within its specific range.

Advanced Techniques and Ornamentation

Once you've mastered the basics, delve into advanced finger techniques and ornamentation. Techniques like trills, grace notes, and slides add flair and expression to your playing. Experiment with these embellishments on familiar tunes to discover how they enhance your musical expression. Advanced fingerings may involve half-holing or uncovering specific holes partially to create nuanced and unique sounds. These techniques contribute to the richness and diversity of your ocarina performances.

Customizing Fingerings for Style

As you progress, consider customizing fingerings to suit your preferred playing style. Different ocarinas and players may find variations in fingerings enhance comfort and control. Experiment with alternative finger placements for specific notes and chords, adjusting them based on your preferences and your music's demands. It not only adds a personal touch to your playing but also allows you to tailor your approach to different genres and musical expressions.

Breathing Techniques and Sound Production

Like a guitarist would use their hands to produce notes, an ocarina player relies on their breath and how well they control it. Start by attentively observing your natural breathing pattern and feeling the expansion and contraction of your ribs and belly.

Slow Exhalation

1. Inhale deeply.

2. While you exhale, produce a constant pitch or a 'hissing' sound.

3. Experiment by gradually slowing down your exhalation, engaging your abdominal muscles slightly.

Fast Exhalation

1. Rhythmically say 'ha' as if you're laughing.

2. Inhale fully, then quickly exhale 'ha,' making sure you engage your chest muscles.

3. Practice exhaling rapidly through a wide-open mouth.

Varied Blowing Speeds

1. Use a metronome or count in your head.

2. Breathe in fully, aiming to expel air in a single metronome click.

3. Repeat, gradually extending the duration with each repetition.

4. Vary blowing pressure, transitioning from slow to fast and vice versa.

Applying to the Ocarina

1. Take your ocarina and finger any note.

2. Smoothly change blowing pressure from very low to high.

3. Notice how the pitch changes and how the ocarina may screech when you blow too hard.

4. Practice playing a scale adjusting pressure for each note.

Breathing Challenges

1. Quickly switch between the lowest and highest pressure.

2. Execute a leap between octaves while aiming to eliminate pitch errors.

3. Practice rapid exhalation and inhalation for improved intonation control.

4. Experiment with 'stepping' inhalation and exhalation while introducing intentional pauses.

Remember, mastering breath control is a gradual process. If you face challenges, ask for advice from flute teachers. They usually have the most experience when it comes to breath control.

Getting the Best Sound Out of Your Ocarina

To get the best sound out of your ocarina's high notes, considering how you're blowing into the instrument is crucial. Follow these steps for optimal results:

Make sure the ocarina is angled correctly without any downward tilting. Hold it straight in front of you with your head up, allowing a smooth airflow.

Avoid

A sharply angled ocarina as it increases turbulence and negatively impacts the tone.

Optimal

Keep the ocarina parallel to the ground for a clear, smooth air passage.

Tongue Position

The position of your tongue plays a significant role in achieving the right sound. Pay attention to your tongue placement to avoid disruptions in airflow.

Avoid

- Raising the back of your tongue can lead to turbulence and a noisy tone.

- Placing the tongue too close to the upper teeth causes turbulence and a disruptive tone.

Optimal

- Keep your tongue in a neutral position for a steady airflow.

Holding Technique:

Hold the ocarina by its ends, keeping all your fingers away from the holes, ensuring an unobstructed airflow. Use a chromatic tuner to check and adjust the pitch while blowing into the ocarina.

If the ocarina produces a good sound after these adjustments, any previous issues with the high notes were likely due to blowing, tongue, or hand posture. However, the ocarina may be the problem if the sound remains poor.

Tips to Improve Your Learning Experience

- **Breath and Airflow**

Craft a unique, pure sound with character by understanding the role of airflow and breath intensity.

- **Material Matters**

Select an ocarina based on its material—clay for warmth, plastic for durability, or metal for a clear, standout tone.

- **The Shape and Size Factor**

Explore how the ocarina's shape and size impact the range of notes it can produce, influencing the overall auditory experience.

- **Environmental Factors**

Observe the instrument's responsiveness to changes in temperature and humidity, adding an element of unpredictability influenced by nature.

- **The Instrument's Voice Box**

Delve into the significance of the voicing, the opening under the mouthpiece, to gain clarity and volume in the sound produced.

- **Holistic Understanding**

Embrace a holistic understanding of the ocarina, incorporating environmental nuances, material choices, and voicing intricacies into your playing.

Chapter 5: Learning Ocarina Songs

Nothing feels as rewarding as finally perfecting a song on an instrument. If you've never played an instrument before, playing a song from start to finish on your ocarina might be very daunting.

9. Perfecting a song on an instrument feels rewarding. Source: https://commons.wikimedia.org/wiki/File:Amerindian_woman_p laying_an_inca_ocarina.png

Luckily, it's not as hard as you might think. If you like a song, you probably know how the tune goes. You can already

---

sing or hear it in your head. If you can, you already know what it's supposed to sound like.

Learning to play your favorite songs on the ocarina is about figuring out how to play the notes. There are different ways to do it:

- **Watch Others**: See how they play and copy their finger movements.

- **By Ear**: Play around with the ocarina, and you'll find patterns that sound like the music you know.

- **Use Sheet Music**: Reading sheet music is easier than you think.

- **Ocarina Tabs**: Online tabs show you where to put your fingers to play a song. You can find them for many popular tunes.

Some ways might be easier for you than others, so try different things to see what works best. Keep in mind that while ocarina tabs are good to start with, they have limits. As you improve, you should try other ways of learning music.

Starting with Simple Melodies

Learning music might seem tricky, but you can make it easier by breaking it into smaller steps. You can rely on two helpful techniques:

1. Break It Down:

Think of your music as a puzzle. Instead of solving the whole puzzle at once, focus on smaller pieces. For example, take the Irish jig "Out on the Ocean." It may seem long, but dividing it into smaller parts makes it easier.

- Start with the first part of the melody. Repeat the finger movements for each segment, getting used to the motions.

- With each try, you'll notice improvement. Move to the next small section when you feel comfortable.

- This step-by-step approach makes learning less overwhelming and builds a strong foundation for mastering the whole piece.

2. Slow It Down:

Adjusting the speed is about giving yourself more time to explore each note. If the original speed is $1/4 = 70$, slow it down. This helps focus on precision before going faster.

- Take your time with each part, paying attention to details.

- As you become more familiar, gradually increase the speed.

- This gradual progress keeps you in control and boosts confidence.

By using these techniques together, even complex pieces become approachable. Practice each part, and combine them to play the entire melody smoothly as you get better. You'll memorize the music and naturally improve your playing speed with consistent practice.

For beginners, there's a wealth of simple melodies you can choose from. These are the most popular, beginner-friendly melodies:

- Twinkle, Twinkle, Little Star

- Mary Had a Little Lamb

- Happy Birthday

- Jingle Bells

- Auld Lange Syne

Progressing to Intermediate Tunes

Playing a Four-Hole Ocarina

To create a variety of sounds on the ocarina is all about learning the art of covering and uncovering the holes with your fingers.

Label and Remember the Holes:

Cover and uncover the four holes with your fingers to make different sounds. Each hole produces a unique pitch, and understanding how to label and remember them is essential to playing your favorite tunes.

- Hold the ocarina like you're about to play and observe the holes.

- Think of the top left hole as "1," top right as "2," bottom left as "3," and bottom right as "4."

- Remember the hole numbers so you can follow instructions easily.

- Use an "x" if a hole should stay uncovered.

For Example:

- Middle C is 1 2 3 4, covering all the holes with your pointer and middle fingers while blowing.

- D is 1 X 3 4, covering all holes except the top right one.

This approach gives you an easy way to understand and play your four-hole ocarina. This labeling trick will be handy as you start getting the hang of playing.

Learning the Basics - Play Your Scales:

Start by getting to know simple scales. Go slow and remember how to use your fingers to make different notes. Don't worry about playing fast right now. Just focus on getting it right. Follow these finger patterns:

- **Middle C:** 1 2 3 4
- **D:** 1 X 3 4
- **E:** 1 2 3 X
- **F:** 1 X 3 X
- **F# (Gb):** X 2 3 4
- **G:** X X 3 4
- **G# (Ab):** X 2 3 X
- **A:** X X 3 X
- **A# (Bb):** X X X 4
- **B:** X 2 X X
- **C:** XXXX

Practice Your Scales:

To get better at playing the ocarina, practice moving up and down these scales. Pay attention to two things:

Remembering Notes and Finger Movements:

- Learn the notes each finger pattern makes. For example, going up a C scale sounds like C-D-E-F-G-A-B-C.

- Memorize these patterns because they're the starting point for many songs.

Speed:

- Try to play faster as you go up and down the scales. Make sure you're getting it right before trying to go too fast.

- The better you get at remembering patterns and playing faster, the more fun you'll have making music with your ocarina.

Playing a Six-Hole Ocarina

Now comes the six-hole Ocarina. It's not much different from the four-hole variation.

Label and Remember the Holes:

Like a four-hole ocarina, you need to memorize how to make different notes. To identify the six holes, follow these steps:

- Take the ocarina and hold it in your mouth as if you were about to play. Examine the openings in the upper part.

- Consider the following: the top left hole is represented by the number 1, the top right by the number 2, the bottom left by the number 3, and the bottom right by the number 4.

- Now consider the openings on the bottom that your thumbs cover. Designate "5" for the left and "6" for the right.

- Remember these labels so you can follow instructions on playing scales.

- Use an "x" if a hole should stay uncovered.

These steps are an easy way to understand and play your six-hole ocarina. This labeling trick will make learning fun and engaging.

Using Your Six-Hole Ocarina to Play Scales:

Similar to the four-hole ocarina, the six-hole ocarina functions with two additional holes on the rear. The primary distinction is that notes are made by covering the bottom two holes and leaving the upper four holes in the same pattern. The scales can be played as follows:

- **Middle C:** 1 2 3 4 5 6
- **D:** 1 X 3 4 5 6
- **E:** 1 2 3 X 5 6
- **F:** 1 X 3 X 5 6
- **F# (Gb):** X 2 3 4 5 6
- **G:** X X 3 4 5 6
- **G# (Ab):** X 2 3 X 5 6
- **A:** X X 3 X 5 6
- **A# (Bb):** X X X 4 5 6
- **B:** X 2 X X 5 6
- **C:** XXXX 5 6

Start off slowly while practicing these patterns, paying attention to the notes. Even with the extra holes, you'll get the hang of it, and soon, you'll be playing many songs on your six-hole ocarina.

Using the Bottom Holes on Your Six-Hole Ocarina:

These holes change the basic notes from before, either going up by one step (a little higher) or by two steps (a bit higher). Here's how to go about it:

- Start with the finger placements for the lower note (as on a four-hole ocarina) to advance up one step; however, cover hole 5 and leave hole 6 uncovered.

- To advance by two steps, begin with the finger positions on a four-hole ocarina for the lower note; however, cover hole 6 and leave hole 5 open.

Understanding this helps you play different notes. A "tone" elevates a note in the scale by two steps (like C to D), whereas a "semitone" raises a note by one step (like C to C#).

For Instance:

- Use holes 1-4 for C (XXXX) to play C#. Then, go up one step by revealing hole 6, leaving only hole 5 covered (X X X 5 X).

- Starting with C (XXXX56), advance ahead two steps to expose hole 5, leaving only hole 6 (X X X X X 6) covered in order to proceed from C to D.

This way, your fingers can move more easily, making it simpler to play different notes.

Playing Your Ocarina Scales:

Here are two important things to consider while practicing scales:

Remembering Notes and Finger Moves:

- Learn the notes for each finger position. For instance, when you play a C scale, it goes C-D-E-F-G-A-B-C.

- Remember these moves because they're the building blocks for many songs you'll play.

Speed:

- Try to play faster as you go up and down the scale. Make sure you're doing it right before trying to go too fast.

- The better you get at remembering moves and playing faster, the more fun you'll have to make music with your ocarina.

Practicing scales is like practicing the ABCs for music. It helps you improve and makes playing songs more enjoyable.

Making music sound good involves a few neat tricks. First, when you play your ocarina, think about how you stop and start the notes. This creates "phrasing." You can make a note to last a long time by stopping the air for a while or make a quick break by stopping it briefly. These breaks help you catch your breath and add a nice touch to the music.

Next, there's "ornamentation," adding unique details to your playing. One easy trick is "vibrato," where you slightly change the pitch of a note by adjusting your blowing pressure. It's like adding a little spice to your music. Other cool ornaments are grace notes, rolls, cranns, and humming into your ocarina.

Changing the loudness of your notes, known as "volume dynamics," can be tricky on the ocarina. Some people use a microphone, while others change how hard they blow and adjust their fingers. But if that sounds complicated, no worries – you can use ornaments like pitch bends or quick flourishes to make your music stand out.

Talking about rhythms. Sometimes, it's fun to play with the timing of your notes. You can play a bit early or a bit late to add excitement or tension to your music. Listen to your favorite songs, and notice how the singers or players do these things. Copying them allows you to create your own rhythms, which, in turn, helps you improve your improvisation skills.

Chapter 6: Ocarina Techniques and Tips

You will learn about vibrato, dynamics, and articulation in this chapter. These add depth to your music and elevate it beyond the norm. You will also learn how you can express feelings through music.

10. There are many techniques to playing the ocarina. Source: GabboT, CC BY-SA 2.0 <https://creativecommons.org/licenses/by-sa/2.0>, via Wikimedia Commons: https://commons.wikimedia.org/wiki/File:Fan_Expo_2012_-_Zelda_(8143151762).jpg

---

Vibrato, Dynamics, and Articulation

Vibrato

Vibrato is a cool trick that adds feeling and variety to your music. It works by gently and quickly changing how you blow into your instrument. While it makes your playing more expressive, it takes a bit of practice to get good at it.

The following are easy tips to learn vibrato.

Start without the Vibrato

Before adding vibrato to your ocarina tunes, practice without it. Take a deep breath, then exhale slowly while making a "ha" sound. Try changing the strength of your breath from soft to loud and back. Use a metronome to keep a steady beat. This exercise helps your muscles get accustomed to vibrato.

Add Vibrato

Pick a comfy note, like middle C on a tenor ocarina. Play the note with a steady breath, and then add vibrato by changing your breath pressure. Begin with a slow and wide vibrato, and, as you become more confident, make it faster and narrower. Play around with different speeds to fit your music's mood.

Vibrato Exercises

To make your vibrato even better, try some exercises. Practice it on different notes, try it with different scales, and see how it sounds. You can use a tuner (a tool that helps you stay on the pitch) or a recorder to check if your notes sound good. Also, play with different ocarinas. You can also practice vibrato on different ocarinas, such as alto, soprano, or bass, to see how they affect your sound and breath.

Learn from Others

Watch videos or recordings of expert ocarina players. Watch how they play and copy them. Ocarina players or teachers can give you tips on how to make your vibrato better and more controlled. Imitate their techniques, comparing them to yours to improve your music.

Practice Finger Moves

Continue playing vibrato by experimenting with finger movements. Change the way you press the finger holes when holding a note. Explore the feelings and sounds created by different finger combinations and actions.

Experiment with Vibrato Speed

Explore different vibrato speeds to find what suits the musical context. Slow, subtle vibrato may work well for certain pieces, while faster vibrato can add intensity.

Identify Finger Movement

Focus on one finger at a time for more control. Move only one finger while holding a note. This isolation approach improves control and precision, allowing you to place the vibrato precisely where you want it. It's similar to teaching each finger its role in the vibrato dance.

Bringing Breath and Finger Vibrato Together

Coordinate your breath and finger movements for a more advanced touch. Test with changing both aspects at the same time to achieve a more detailed and layered vibrato effect. This combination provides a dynamic aspect to your vibrato signature, allowing you to create your own.

Keep Practicing and Have Fun

Keep practicing, and don't worry if it's not perfect at first. Enjoy the process, and soon you'll notice your tunes becoming more magical and full of emotion. So, keep playing, keep practicing, and let the enchanting sound of vibrato make your music even more special.

Dynamics

Dynamics is like turning the volume up and down in your ocarina music. It makes your tunes exciting by going from soft to loud and back again. It might sound tricky, but with a bit of practice, you'll make your ocarina sing with emotion.

Here are easy tips to bring your music to life using dynamics.

Soft and Loud Moments

Dynamics is volume control for your ocarina. It allows you to play softly one moment and very loud the next. It makes your music interesting and fun to listen to.

Try with Simple Tunes

Start by practicing dynamics with songs you already know. Play a part of the song quietly, then loudly. Switch it up for different parts of the tune.

Tongue Tricks, Starting and Ending Notes

Use your tongue to start and end each note differently. Try short and bouncy, long and smooth, or with a little emphasis.

Changing the Pitch

Your fingers are the pitch controllers. Covering more holes makes the sound lower, and covering fewer holes make it higher. Experiment with different finger moves, like sliding or bending.

Connect with Music

Let your emotions guide you. Imagine you're telling a story with your ocarina. Feel the happiness or sadness in the music, and let your ocarina reflect those feelings. If it's a happy part, play it loud and joyful. If it's a quiet, reflective moment, keep it soft.

Record Yourself

Record your ocarina playing on your phone. Listen to it and see how your dynamics sound.

Play with Speed

Change the volume at different speeds. Some tunes sound great with slow changes, while others might need quick shifts.

Articulation

When you play the ocarina, you want each part of your music to sound unique. One way to do this is by how you start and connect the notes – called "articulation." Since it's a bit tricky to control the loudness and tone, only focus on how you start and stop the notes.

Here's a simple tip: start each group of notes by gently touching your tongue to the ocarina for the first note. Then, for the rest of the notes in that group, smoothly connect them without using your tongue. If there are notes that sound the same, use a softer and quicker tongue touch to separate them.

Imagine you're saying "ta" for the first note and then letting the other notes flow smoothly.

Articulation Exercises

Focus on articulation with exercises such as playing scales using staccato (short and detached) and legato (smooth and connected) techniques. This improves finger control.

Use Articulation Marks:

Pay close attention to articulation marks in sheet music. Properly execute symbols like staccato dots or legato lines to follow the composer's intentions.

Tips for Articulation:

- **Start Slow: Saying "Ta" or "Da":** Practice saying "ta" or "da" softly to gently start each note. Start slow, get comfy, and then go a bit faster. This makes your notes sound crisp and clear.

- **"T" Is for Quick and Sharp:** Use the tip of your tongue. Touch the roof of your mouth behind your teeth and release quickly while blowing into the ocarina.

- **"Kah" Is for Soft and Round:** Use the back of your tongue. Touch the soft palate and release while blowing. This creates a smooth and round sound, perfect for those gentle, flowing moments.

- **"T-Kah" for a Rolling Effect:** Switch between "T" and "Kah." Roll your tongue for effect.

- **Finger Tricks for Variety:** Get creative with your fingers. Slide, bend, or half-hole the finger holes. It's like painting with different colors, adding unique touches to your musical canvas.

- **Listen and Copy:** Check out other ocarina players. Listen to how they play and copy their moves.

- **Practice Regularly:** Keep practicing. Make it a regular habit to keep your moves sharp.

Expressing Emotion through Your Playing

Expressing emotions through music on the ocarina is a deeply personal and enriching experience. With its unique timbre and expressive capabilities, the ocarina is a powerful vessel for conveying a wide range of emotions. Each note played carries the potential to evoke feelings of joy, sorrow, excitement, or contemplation. To truly express emotions, a player must develop an intimate connection with the instrument, transcending technical proficiency to infuse each melody with genuine sentiment.

The ocarina's versatility allows for various techniques, such as vibrato, dynamics, and articulation, which can be employed to shape the emotional landscape of a piece. Slow, soulful tunes may embrace subtle vibrato and legato phrasing to convey melancholy. Lively compositions might incorporate staccato articulation and dynamic contrasts for a sense of jubilation. Experimenting with breath control and exploring the instrument's tonal range enables the ocarina player to mirror the complexity of human emotions.

The nuances of tempo, phrasing, and tonal variations play a major role in accurately translating feelings into music. By meticulously interpreting the composer's intentions, you can channel a wide spectrum of emotions, from the serene tranquility of a slow adagio to the exuberant energy of an allegro. Embracing the inherent expressiveness of the ocarina allows you to communicate sentiments that resonate with you and your audience, creating a shared emotional experience through the universal language of music.

Your ocarina creates different sounds based on how hard you blow into it, but it sounds just right at a specific blowing pressure for each set of finger positions. While you can technically adjust the volume, most of the expressive magic happens through how you play with the notes and add decorations. Playing the ocarina is like painting a colorful picture of emotions through your music. It's not only about getting the notes right. It's about expressing feelings.

Here are easy ways to make your ocarina playing truly emotional:

- **Soft and Loud Moments:** Play some parts soft and others loud. This adds emotion - soft for quiet moments and loud for strong feelings. It's like adjusting the volume of your emotions.

- **Different Ways to Speak:** Experiment with how you play each note. Play short and bouncy for happy moments or smooth and connected for calm ones.

- **Breath as Your Storyteller:** Your breath is your music storyteller. Practice different ways of breathing to make your playing intense or calm.

- **Power of Pauses:** Take breaks between notes. Pauses are like musical commas, adding suspense or reflection. Like in a good story, pauses make your music more interesting.

- **Tell a Story with Your Notes:** Play your notes differently. Experiment with short and snappy or smooth and connected.

Your ocarina's pitch isn't always steady, and that's completely fine. You can shake up the sound by making some notes wobble (vibrato). Playing with the pitch rhythmically can suggest a beat, and tweaking the note's pitch on purpose can add tension to your music.

Chapter 7: Playing Along with Others

Playing with fellow musicians introduces a new dimension to your ocarina adventure. It's a collaborative venture where your individual melodies intertwine, creating a tapestry of sound that transcends the capabilities of a single instrument. Whether you're engaging in duets, joining an ensemble, or participating in a larger musical group, this chapter provides insights into the dynamics of group play, fostering connections and enhancing your musical journey.

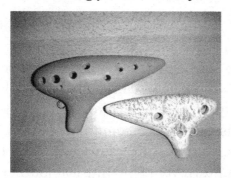

11. Playing the ocarina with others can offer you many benefits.
Source: user:朝彦, Public domain, via Wikimedia Commons:
https://commons.wikimedia.org/wiki/File:Ocarina_SopranoF_Alt
oC.jpg

Joining Ocarina Communities

Joining ocarina communities offers a multitude of benefits for enthusiasts of this unique instrument. Firstly, it provides a platform for connecting with like-minded individuals who share a passion for the ocarina. Whether you're a beginner looking for guidance or an experienced player eager to share insights, these communities create a supportive environment for mutual learning and growth. The collective knowledge within these groups is a valuable resource that can enhance your playing skills and deepen your understanding of the instrument.

Another advantage of joining ocarina communities is the opportunity for collaboration. Engaging with fellow players allows you to embark on musical projects, share compositions, and collaborate on performances. This collaborative spirit fosters creativity and opens doors to new and exciting possibilities, like group performances, virtual collaborations, or themed musical projects. The diverse backgrounds and experiences of community members contribute to a rich tapestry of ideas and create a vibrant space for artistic exploration.

Beyond the realm of music, ocarina communities often extend into discussions about instrument maintenance, purchasing advice, and various aspects of ocarina culture. Whether discovering new ocarina models, exploring different playing techniques, or delving into the instrument's historical and cultural aspects, these communities provide a platform for broadening your ocarina knowledge. Also, being part of a community can turn your solo musical journey into a shared adventure as you celebrate successes, navigate challenges, and forge connections with fellow ocarina enthusiasts around the world.

Why Play in a Group

Playing the ocarina as part of a group is an immensely enjoyable experience that adds layers of fun and fulfillment to your musical journey. The magic unfolds as individual ocarinas come together, creating a harmonious blend of sounds that transcends the capabilities of a solo performance. The synergy achieved in a group setting offers a rich and textured musical tapestry, where each instrument contributes a unique voice to the collective melody. Whether you're part of a small ensemble or a larger musical group, the shared camaraderie and the joy of creating music together amplify the pleasure of playing the ocarina.

One of the most rewarding aspects of group play is the sense of connection it fosters among musicians. As you synchronize your playing with others, you forge bonds of musical understanding and cooperation. The shared experience of interpreting a piece, responding to cues, and collectively adjusting dynamics creates a sense of unity and shared achievement. Group play introduces an element of spontaneity, where musicians can respond to each other's nuances, creating a dynamic and interactive musical dialogue.

Why You Should Try Playing in a Group:

1. **Shared Joy:** Experiencing the joy of collectively bringing a piece to life is a unique and rewarding aspect of group play. Shared achievements like mastering a challenging passage or delivering a captivating performance contribute to a sense of accomplishment that is deeply satisfying and memorable.

2. **Learning Together**: Playing in a group provides valuable learning opportunities. Interacting with fellow musicians allows you to observe different playing styles, techniques, and interpretations.

Learning from others and receiving constructive feedback can significantly contribute to your musical growth.

3. **Dynamic Musical Dialogue:** Group play introduces a dynamic musical dialogue. Musicians can respond to each other's expressions, nuances, and improvisations in real-time, creating a dynamic and interactive performance. This spontaneity adds an exciting dimension to the musical experience.

What's Your Preferred Learning Style?

Some individuals thrive in solitary, self-directed learning environments, relishing the freedom to set their own pace and structure. Learning on your own provides the flexibility to explore the instrument independently, tailoring your practice sessions to suit your unique needs and preferences. With an abundance of online resources and tutorials, self-directed learners can choose their curriculum, delve into specific topics of interest, and progress at their own speed. This approach can be especially beneficial for those who enjoy the autonomy of crafting their musical journey.

On the other hand, group learning offers a dynamic and interactive experience that can significantly enhance your ocarina skills. Joining a group, whether in-person or online, introduces an element of camaraderie and shared enthusiasm. Collaborating with fellow learners provides opportunities for peer feedback, collective problem-solving, and a sense of community. Group settings often involve structured lessons, workshops, and shared practice sessions, fostering a supportive environment that can boost motivation and accountability. Engaging with others who share a passion for the ocarina can be inspiring, offering fresh perspectives, insights, and the chance to learn from different playing styles.

Ultimately, the choice between learning on your own or in a group depends on your personal preferences, goals, and the type of learning experience that resonates most with you.

Collaborating with Musicians and Ensembles

What to Expect from Collaborating with Others

Being in a group makes learning much more exciting. Ensembles help you not only get better at playing but also let you enjoy making music together. You and your peers work together, figuring out how to play your ocarinas with other instruments.

Playing with other musicians and groups is not only about getting better at your ocarina. You get to perform in front of people, showing off your ocarina skills to a bigger crowd. The excitement of performing alongside others is unlike anything else. It helps you improve at being on stage, match your playing with others, and feel the joy of achieving things together.

You share ideas, tricks, and creative ways to play in a group. When you play with musicians who use other instruments, you have the chance to learn different techniques, melodies, and styles you can use in your playing.

When exploring playing ocarina with others, think about joining groups online or in your neighborhood. Online, you can connect with players from all around the world, making friends without worrying about the distance. If you prefer being with people in person, joining a local group means you can collaborate face-to-face, creating a strong bond with your musical friends.

On November 5, 2013, something memorable took place at the Royal Albert Hall. During the annual Barnardo's Young

Supporters' Concert, a group of 3,081 kids and adults broke the world record for the largest group of people playing ocarinas together. The previous record was held by 831 players in China.

They played a song called "Ode to a Joyful Star" under the guidance of a famous composer, Douglas Coombes. They even had the Grand Organ in the hall playing along with them.

2013 was a special year for the ocarina, celebrating 50 years since the English 4-hole Ocarina was invented, 30 years of the Ocarinas in the UK Schools program, and 25 years of the English Plastic Ocarina.

This event not only set a world record but also raised over £40,000 for Barnardo's Young Supporters.

Benefits of Collaborating with Other Musicians

The journey of learning to play the ocarina is often more rewarding when shared with others. Joining Ocarina communities provides a platform for mutual support and encouragement, creating a shared space for learners to exchange insights and experiences. Being part of a community allows you to tap into a collective pool of knowledge, with seasoned players offering guidance to those taking their first steps. A sense of camaraderie develops through shared challenges and triumphs, turning the learning process into a collaborative adventure.

Groups and ensembles offer an environment where players of all skill levels can come together to learn, practice, and inspire each other. Whether you're a beginner seeking guidance or an experienced player looking to share your expertise, these communities provide a diverse and inclusive space. Engaging with fellow ocarina enthusiasts exposes you to different playing styles, techniques, and musical genres, broadening your musical horizons. Learning from peers with varied experiences adds depth to your musical journey, allowing you to explore new facets of ocarina playing.

Apart from skill development, being part of an ocarina community offers a sense of belonging. The shared passion for this unique instrument creates lasting connections and friendships.

Performance Opportunities and Community Engagement

Collaborating with fellow musicians and ensembles offers a plethora of benefits, extending beyond personal skill development. Showcasing your ocarina skills in ensembles provides a unique avenue for gaining exposure within your local community. Whether participating in a chamber ensemble or joining forces with other instrumentalists, these performances become opportunities to shine and connect with a broader audience. The shared experience of making music together fosters a sense of camaraderie and mutual support.

Beyond personal growth, engaging in ensemble performances plays a vital role in building confidence and stage presence. Facing an audience as part of a group helps alleviate performance anxiety and allows musicians to feed off the collective energy of the ensemble. This collaborative setting not only refines technical abilities but also nurtures essential interpersonal skills, as effective communication becomes vital to a cohesive and harmonious performance.

The joy of music is magnified when shared, and participating in ensembles provides the chance to contribute to the broader musical community. Whether it's a local band, orchestra, or chamber group, your ocarina playing becomes a valuable addition to the collective artistic expression. These collaborative efforts not only enrich the cultural landscape of your community but also contribute to the diversity and vibrancy of musical experiences.

Finally, collaborating with other musicians in ensembles fosters connections and deepens the appreciation for music. Sharing the stage with diverse instruments and voices opens new possibilities for musical exploration. The blend of tones and textures in ensemble playing creates a rich sonic tapestry, enhancing the overall listening experience. As you engage in these collaborative endeavors, you refine your ocarina skills and contribute to a harmonious and interconnected musical world.

Chapter 8: Advancing Your Ocarina Skills

In this final chapter, you'll learn how to play by ear and tackle more complex tunes. You'll also understand pitch patterns, play simple melodies, and adapt music for your ocarina. This chapter closes by sharing easy ways to record and share your music online.

12. There are many ways to advance your ocarina skills. Source: Patian, CC BY-SA 3.0 <https://creativecommons.org/licenses/by-sa/3.0>, via Wikimedia Commons: https://commons.wikimedia.org/wiki/File:Ocarina_4.JPG

Exploring More Complex Pieces: Playing the Ocarina by Ear

Contrary to common belief, playing the ocarina by ear is not an innate skill but rather a learned ability. It's comparable to dealing with a foreign language. You might recognize certain patterns in the sound, yet understanding the meaning comes with learning the words and grammar.

Understanding Pitch Patterns

Much like a language, music consists of patterns: a melody is a sequence of notes with different pitches, forming larger structures called figures and phrases. Playing the ocarina by ear involves recognizing and reproducing these patterns on your instrument.

Observing Pitch Differences:

- Moving from low to medium and from low to high sounds different.

- Moving from low to high differs from moving from high to low despite using the same pitches.

- Consecutively playing the same note has a distinct sound.

These observations form the basis for recognizing pitch patterns and learning to play by ear.

Playing a Simple Melody

Form a melody using these three notes. For instance:

- Low, Low, Medium, Low, Low, Medium, High, Low

Identifying Note Movements:

- A sequence of notes at the same pitch (e.g., Low, Low, Low).

- An ascending sequence (e.g., Low, Medium, High).

- A descending sequence (e.g., High, Medium, Low).

- A leap: Low to High or High to Low, skipping Medium.

Listening to Melodies

Playing by ear is a three-step process:

- **Listen to the Notes**: Listen to the three notes and remember their pitches and how they sound.

- **Listen to the Melody**: Listen to the whole melody without playing. Memorize the structure and note the pitch changes.

- **Play**: Play the notes and listen. Does it sound the same?

Applying It to the Ocarina

Now, play it on the Ocarina. Familiarize yourself with the range of notes, then practice playing random melodies. Increase the range gradually as you gain experience.

Tips:

- Play all the notes on your ocarina to understand their sound.

- Listen to the entire melody and visualize the pitch changes.

- Practice playing different melodies, not only the ones you're comfortable with.

Playing Rhythm by Ear

While most people can easily copy rhythm by ear, it's crucial to do it accurately.

Choosing Music for Your Ocarina

When choosing music for your ocarina, you often adapt pieces made for other instruments or voices. There's not a lot of music specifically written for the ocarina yet. Most of it comes from the Italian ocarina septet tradition, and you can find some original compositions online.

Adapting music means thinking about the ocarina's limited range and fixed timbre. Like the alto C, single-chambered ocarinas have about an octave and a fourth in range. It can be shifted up or down by changing the key, but it might affect the sound quality of some notes.

Unlike many other instruments, one ocarina can't cover all musical aspects. Due to its range and timbre limits, players often need multiple ocarinas for different purposes.

Adapting vocal music to single-chambered ocarinas is easier because of their similar range to untrained human voices. Folk tunes, especially bagpipe music, also work well with the ocarina.

Multi-chamber ocarinas can cover more range, but they have challenges. Splitting the range and dealing with finger complexity in certain keys can make some expressive possibilities tricky.

How Ocarina Music Is Written

Ocarina music is usually written using standard notation. Since it has less than two octaves, notes are simply called 'high' and 'low,' like 'high C' and 'Low C.'

The low C on the staff is considered 'low C' on the ocarina, even if it sounds higher. For example, an alto C ocarina sounds an octave higher than written.

Some instruments transpose their notation into C for ease, but not all ocarina players do this. Ensemble music often uses the treble clef, even for bass and contrabass ocarinas.

Learning to read music at a written pitch in different keys is useful as it lets you play various music without transposing it first. This skill is handy for pieces written for other instruments or voices.

Folk music, like Scottish bagpipe tunes, suits the ocarina well. It's usually written at a sounding pitch, making the skill of reading at written pitch across different keys quite helpful.

Advanced Pieces to Try

Whether you're a fan of fantasy themes, classic cinema, or traditional tunes, there's a vast repertoire waiting to be explored on your ocarina.

- **"Song of Time" from The Legend of Zelda: Ocarina of Time:**

As an iconic tune from the beloved video game, this melody is a must for any ocarina player. Its enchanting notes will transport you to the mystical world of Hyrule.

- **"Concerning Hobbits" from The Lord of the Rings:**

Capture the essence of the Shire with this whimsical and heartwarming melody. The ocarina's sweet tones beautifully convey the simple and pastoral atmosphere of Tolkien's world.

- **"Over the Rainbow" from The Wizard of Oz:**

With its timeless melody, this classic song is perfect for showcasing the ocarina's ability to evoke emotion.

Experiment with dynamics and vibrato to add your touch to this beloved tune.

- **"My Heart Will Go On" from Titanic:**

Let the ocarina express the romantic and haunting quality of this cinematic masterpiece. The instrument's versatility shines as you navigate through the emotional highs and lows of the melody.

- **"Simple Gifts" (Traditional Shaker Hymn):**

Explore the simplicity and beauty of this traditional hymn, allowing the ocarina's pure tones to resonate. Its straightforward melody provides an excellent opportunity to focus on expression and dynamics in your playing.

- **"Somewhere Over the Rainbow" by Israel Kamakawiwo'ole:**

Embrace the ukulele-infused rendition of this classic and adapt it to your ocarina. The soothing island vibes and gentle melody provide an opportunity to experiment with your ocarina's tonal range and articulation.

- **"Game of Thrones Theme" by Ramin Djawadi:**

Dive into the epic world of Westeros by playing the iconic Game of Thrones theme on your ocarina. The haunting melody and dramatic undertones will let you explore the instrument's ability to capture the essence of a powerful soundtrack.

Recording and Sharing Your Ocarina Music

Recording and sharing your ocarina music opens up a world of possibilities for personal growth and connecting with a wider audience. This section explores the steps to capture your performances and how to share them with the world.

When you listen to your recordings, you can see how much you're improving. Plus, when you share your music, you get helpful feedback from others.

Another great thing is that it connects you with a community of other musicians. You become friends with people who love the ocarina just like you. You share your tunes and hear theirs.

Recording your music can be a motivation boost, too. Knowing that others might enjoy what you play pushes you to keep getting better. It's also a way of expressing feelings and telling stories through your ocarina.

To start recording your music, you need to:

- **Select the Right Equipment:**

Before you dive into recording, choosing the right equipment is essential. Consider investing in a quality microphone and audio interface to ensure the best sound quality. Experiment with different setups to find the one that suits your preferences and the style of your ocarina playing. The goal is to capture the nuances and dynamics of your music accurately.

- **Master Sound Production:**

Recording an ocarina involves more than just pressing the record button. Learn the basics of sound production, including adjusting microphone placement, understanding equalization, and applying reverb or other effects. This knowledge allows you to enhance the clarity and richness of your ocarina tones during the recording process.

- **Familiarize Yourself with Recording Techniques:**

Explore various recording techniques to find what works best for your ocarina style. Consider multi-track recording to layer different ocarina parts or experimenting with live recordings to capture the raw energy of your performances. Pay attention to room acoustics and ambient noise, making adjustments to create a clean and polished recording. With these techniques, you can create professional-sounding ocarina tracks that reflect your unique musical expression.

- **How to Effectively Record Your Ocarina**

If you want to record yourself playing the ocarina, whether to share it or merely to listen and improve, here are simple tips for getting the best sound.

Recording Equipment Basics:

- The microphones in phones and laptops are not great for musical instruments like the ocarina.

- You need a special microphone for better sound quality.

Options for Recording:

Portable Audio Recorders:

- These are all-in-one devices with built-in microphones.

- Easy to use – just press record.

- Suitable for beginners and recording on the go.

- Look for ones designed for recording music, like the Zoom H1.

USB Microphones:

- Connect these directly to your computer.

- Simple and efficient for amateur recording.

- Better sound quality than built-in microphones.

XLR Microphones:

- These provide the best sound quality but are a bit more complex.

- Need additional equipment like an XLR cable and interface.

- Great if you're serious about recording.

Important Note:

- Some microphones need 'phantom power,' so check if your equipment supports it.

If you want something easy, go for a portable recorder or a USB microphone. If you want the best quality and don't mind some complexity, consider an XLR microphone. Choose what suits your needs and budget.

Sharing Your Ocarina Music

Now that you've recorded your ocarina music, learn about sharing it with others:

- **Make a SoundCloud or YouTube Channel:** Create an account on SoundCloud or YouTube to upload your music. These sites allow people from all over to hear what you've played.

- **Share on Social Media:** Use Instagram, Facebook, or Twitter to share your music with more people. Share your recordings and connect with other musicians and ocarina lovers.

- **Join Ocarina Groups Online:** Be part of online Ocarina groups. Share your music, ask for tips, and talk to others who love the ocarina. Websites like The Ocarina Network and Reddit's r/Ocarina are great places to join.

- **Play with Other Musicians:** Make music with people who play other instruments. This can create cool and different music.

- **Join Challenges and Contests:** Some online groups have fun challenges. Participate in these events to show your skills, get advice, and challenge yourself to improve.

Conclusion

Now that you have reached the end of this book, reflect on what you learned, and don't hesitate to leave a review. From understanding the rich background of this magical instrument to choosing the perfect ocarina that resonates with your soul, you've embraced the artistry that lies within its delicate curves and intricate voicings.

The exploration of basic music theory has laid a sturdy foundation, empowering you to read musical notations easily. You've honed your skills in handling the ocarina, mastering proper hand positions and fingerings that bring forth the melodies effortlessly. Learning ocarina songs became more than just playing notes; it transformed into a means of expressing your emotions and stories through the enchanting tunes.

Venturing into the realm of ocarina techniques and artistry elevated your playing to new heights. Vibrato, dynamics, and articulation became not only technicalities but also tools through which you convey the depth and nuances of your musical expressions. Playing with others added a harmonious dimension, fostering connections with fellow musicians and creating musical synergy.

As you advanced your ocarina skills, delving into intricate compositions and mastering advanced techniques, you became a storyteller through sound. The ocarina, once a mere instrument, evolved into an extension of your emotions, translating the language of your heart into melodies that resonate with others.

This book has been written to encourage, challenge, and inspire. But your ocarina adventure doesn't end here. It's an ever-evolving symphony of discovery. Whether you're playing for yourself, with friends, or in front of an audience, may the melodies you create bring joy, inspiration, and a touch of magic to those who listen.

With the knowledge gained and the skills developed, you now hold the key to unlocking limitless possibilities with your ocarina. This is not an end but a new beginning. So, let the echoes of your ocarina reverberate through time, and may your musical journey continue to unfold with every breath, every note, and every enchanting melody.

Although often overlooked in the symphony of musical instruments, the ocarina stands as a silent staple with a profound ability to captivate hearts. Its unassuming appearance conceals a world of musical versatility, capable of producing ethereal melodies that weave through the air like whispers of a forgotten tale. Despite its modest size, its silent presence resonates with a certain charm, drawing listeners into its enchanting sphere.

In gatherings and musical ensembles, the ocarina may be considered a silent hero, waiting for its moment to emerge and add a distinctive voice to the harmony. Its unique tonal qualities, ranging from hauntingly sweet to joyously uplifting, make it an invaluable addition to any musical composition. Its ability to seamlessly blend with various instruments, whether traditional or contemporary, elevates its status as a silent staple that can enhance the emotional depth of a musical arrangement. As you continue your journey with the ocarina, you'll discover its power to communicate profound emotions.

References

Fosdick, H. (n.d.). Beginner's Guide to the Ocarina.Flute Tunes.
https://www.flutetunes.com/articles/ocarina/

Liggins, D., & Liggins, C. (n.d.). About Us. Ocarina.
https://www.ocarina.co.uk/about-

Ocarina | Art Sphere Inc. (2022, September 16). Art Sphere Inc.
https://artsphere.org/ocarina/

Ocarinas of the Americas: Music Made in Clay. (n.d.). Peabody Museum
of Archaeology and Ethnology. https://peabody.harvard.edu/OE-
ocarinas-americas

Pure Ocarinas. (n.d.). Concert quality ocarinas designed for the player.
Pure Ocarinas. https://pureocarinas.com/index

Made in the USA
Las Vegas, NV
23 November 2024

12477675R00049